TEST OF ESSENTIAL ACADEMIC SKILLS (TEAS)

ENGLISH LANGUAGE

1. Many prefer donating money _____ distributing clothes.

   a) To
   b) On
   c) In
   d) But

Answer: a

2. Choose the Antonym for 'Plaintiff'

   a) Complainant
   b) Sorrowful
   c) Defendant
   d) Witness

Answer: a

3. Choose the right Preposition for the blank:

   I am not good _____ translation

   a) At
   b) In .
   c) For
   d) With

Answer: a

1

MAY 1 4 2013

4. Which word is correctly spelled?

a) Blasfami
b) Blusphemi
c) Blasfemi
d) Blasphemy

Answer: d

5. Three fourths of the work _____ finished.

a) Have been
b) Had
c) Has
d) Has been

Answer: d

6. Choose the correct Synonym for the word 'Extempore'

a) Improvise
b) Immediate
c) Planned
d) Impromptu

Answer: d

7. When one is pragmatic, he is being _____.

a) Wasteful
b) Practical

c) Productive

d) Fussy

Answer: b

8. The word bounty is closest in meaning to _____

a) Familiar

b) Generosity

c) Dividing line

d) Sympathy

Answer: b

9. Choose the correct Antonym for 'Cynical'

a) Pessimistic

b) Gullible

c) Equivocal

d) Liberal

Answer: b

10. Choose the word opposite in meaning to the word 'Amicable'

a) Interesting

b) Loving

c) Affectionate

d) Friendly

Answer: d

11. Choose the correctly spelt word

3

a) Volantory
b) Voluntary
c) Voluntery
d) Vulontory

Answer: b

12. Choose the correctly spelt word

a) Accilerate
b) Accelerate
c) Accelerrate
d) Accilarate

Answer: b

13. Choose the correct sentence

a) It is raining for 3 days
b) It has been raining for 3 days
c) It rained for 3 days
d) It was raining for 3 days

Answer: b

14. Just now he _____ his dinner but he says he'll see you when he's finished

a) Is having
b) Has had
c) Was having
d) Had

Answer: b

4

15. She told me his name after he _____.

a) Left
b) Had left
c) Has left
d) Has been leaving

Answer: b

16. Choose the correct sentence

a) I have looked for a doctor before I met you
b) I had looked for a doctor before I met you
c) I looked for a doctor before I had met you
d) I am looking for a doctor before meeting you

Answer: b

17. Do not make a noise while your father _____

a) Is sleeping
b) Has slept
c) Asleep
d) Is being asleep

Answer: a

18. My uncle arrived while I _____ the dinner.

a) Would cook
b) Had cooked

c) Cook

d) Was cooking

Answer: d

19. 'A bird's eye view means-

a) At the last moment

b) A rough idea

c) Very soon

d) A birds vision

Answer: b

20. 'Carry the day' means-

a) Carrying the daily activities

b) Gossip

c) Win

d) Retire

Answer: c

21. 'Go to the dogs' means-

a) Serving the dogs

b) Be ruined

c) Having a dog

d) Behaving rude

Answer: b

22. 'At the eleventh hour' means-

a) Before twelve o'clock
b) At the last moment
c) A sacred hour
d) None of the above

Answer: b

23. 'Loaves and fishes' means-

a) A bag of groceries
b) Personal gains
c) Personal skills
d) A loaf and a fish

Answer: b

24. 'Down to earth' means-

a) Attack on earth
b) An earthly matter
c) Realistic
d) Emotional

Answer: c

25. 'A bolt from the blue' means-

a) An unexpected calamity
b) A blue bolt
c) Time unused
d) None of the above

Answer: a

7

SCIENCE

1. The Human skull is made of ____ different bones

a) 41
b) 29
c) 23
d) 15

Answer: b

2. The Mitochondria contains _____% of Protein

a) 40
b) 87
c) 70
d) It doesn't contain Protein

Answer: c

3. A solid mixture containing a non-volatile component can be separated into its components by the following experimental technique:

a) Solvent extraction
b) Sublimation
c) Crystallization
d) Chromatography

Answer: b

4. Burning of wood is an example of an exothermic reaction. In such reactions, heat of systems _____ during reaction:

a) Decreases
b) Increases
c) Does nothing
d) Reaction does not involve heat production

Answer: b

5. When Electrons are passed through a magnetic field, they are acted upon by the field. The force applied on them bends towards _____

a) North Pole
b) South Pole
c) The path does not bend at all at any Poles
d) Both Poles

Answer: c

6. Why is soft iron used in making Calling bells?

a) Because it rings louder
b) Because it is cheap
c) Because soft iron can easily be turned to magnet
d) Because soft iron is found everywhere

Answer: c

7. What material is used in the memory tape of a Tape Recorder and a computer?

a) Ceramic magnet
b) Normal magnet
c) Iron
d) None of the above

Answer: a

8. The Human body consists of _____ number of bones

a) 350
b) 100
c) 503
d) 206

Answer: d

9. Which of the following vitamins are fat soluble?

a) Vitamin A, D, C
b) Vitamin B Complex and k
c) Vitamin C and D
d) Vitamin D, E and K

Answer: d

10. What are the 3 prime colors?

a) Yellow, brown and red
b) Red, green and blue
c) Pink, orange and green
d) Violet, black and burgundy

Answer: b

11. The word 'Biology' is a/an _____ word

a) Spanish
b) English
c) Greek
d) Italian

Answer: c

12. The gas _____ is made from the fermentation of animal and plant waste

a) Hydrogen
b) Oxygen
c) Helium
d) Methane

Answer: d

13. **'ICBN'** refers to-

a) International Code of Botanical Nomenclature
b) Intermediate college of Botanical Norms
c) International Criminal Book Narration
d) Ideologically clustered Botanical Nomenclature

Answer: a

14. What is a soluble?

a) Something that dissolves in a solution?
b) Something that is mixed in salt?
c) A material that is a solution itself?
d) All of the above

Answer: a

15. What is the main element used in making glass?

a) Magnets
b) Iron
c) Sand/Silica
d) Soft rubber

Answer: c

16. Carolus linius wrote which of the following Books?

a) A Midsummer Nights' Dream
b) A Tale of Two Cities
c) System of Nature
d) A Brief History of Time

Answer: c

17. What is the normal temperature of a Human body?

a) 95.6 F
b) 98.4 F
c) 36.5 F
d) 79.7 F

Answer: b

18. What is the normal volume of blood in a Human?

   a) 4-5 liters
   b) 2-3 liters
   c) 5-6 liters
   d) 8-10 liters

Answer: c

19. Which hormone is responsible for the feminine characteristics?

   a) Insulin
   b) Estrogen
   c) Both a and b
   d) None of the above

Answer: b

20. What is the water quantity in Plasma?

   a) 72-90%
   b) 91-92%
   c) 75-90%
   d) 90-100%

Answer: b

21. Which is the hardest/ strongest part in a Human body?

a) Skull
b) Stomach
c) Limbs
d) Enamel

Answer: d

22. What is the normal heart rate?

a) 85
b) 65
c) 72
d) 79

Answer: c

23. Which of the following gases obstructs the flow of oxygen in blood?

a) Carbon-di-oxide
b) Carbon-Monoxide
c) Cloro-Fluoro Carbon
d) Hydrogen

Answer: b

24. During crystallization, the hot filtered solution is cooled at a moderate rate. This precaution is taken so that-

a) Small size crystals are formed.
b) Big sized crystals are formed
c) Medium sized crystals are formed
d) Microscopic sized crystals are formed

Answer: c

25. The chemical behavior of an Atom is determined by its-

a) Binding energy
b) Mass number
c) Atomic number
d) Number of Isotopes

Answer: c

MATHS

1. The cost of renting a small bus for a trip was $X, which was to be shared equally by 16 people. Actually, 10 people availed the trip. How much will the cost increase for each person?

a) X/6
b) X/10
c) X/40
d) 3X/80

Answer: d

2. A map has a scale of 1cm to 3 km , what length on actual does the 2 cm length on the map represent?

a) 9 km
b) 1 km
c) 6 km
d) 6 cm

Answer: c

3. If 'p' is an even integer, and 'q' is an odd integer, which of the following must be an odd integer?

a) p/q
b) 2p+q
c) pq
d) 2(p+q)

Answer: d

4. If a light flashes every 6 seconds, how many times will it flash in ¾ of an hour?

a) 450 times
b) 449 times
c) 451 times
d) 550 times

Answer: a

5. If 6 and X have the same mean as 2,4 and 24, what is the value of X?

a) 5
b) 10
c) 14
d) 36

Answer: c

6. How much is the value -4- (-10) greater than the value of -10-(-4)?

a) 0
b) 6
c) 14
d) 12

Answer: d

7. Consider the following series: 3, 4, 6, 9, 13, ____ what comes next?

a) 15
b) 16
c) 17
d) 18

Answer: d

8. How much interest will $1 earn in one year at an annual interest rate of 20% if interest rate is compounded every 6 months?

a) 200
b) 205
c) 110
d) 210

Answer: d

9. If the length of a rectangle is increased by 30%, and the width is increased by 30%, then the area of the rectangle will be-

a) Decreased by 9%
b) Increased by 16%
c) Increased by 9%
d) Increased by 15%

Answer: a

10. The average mark in Maths in a class of 40 students is 45. Average mark of all 30 boys is 50. Then how much would the average mark obtained by the girls be?

a) 30
b) 35
c) 25
d) 40

Answer: a

11. 729 ml of a mixture contains milk and water in ratio 7:2 how much of the water is to be added to get a new mixture containing half milk and half water?

a) 405ml
b) 81ml
c) 72ml
d) 91ml

Answer: a

12. The sum of 3 consecutive odd numbers is 57.the middle one is _____

a) 19
b) 21
c) 23
d) 17

Answer: a

13. In a box, there are 8 red, 7 blue and 6 green balls. One ball is picked up randomly. What is the probability that it is neither red nor green?

a) 1/3
b) 3/4
c) 7/19
d) 8/21

Answer: a

14. Mr. A has won an election by a vote of 250-150. What part of the total vote was against him?

a) 2/5
b) 3/5
c) 4/7
d) 3/8

Answer: d

15. In a city, 90% of the population owns a car, 15% own a Motorbike and everybody owns one or the other or both. What is the percentage of Motorbike owners who also owns a car?

a) 5%
b) 15%
c) 33.33%
d) 50%

Answer: c

16. There are 3600 employees in ABC Ltd. One third are clerical, if they were to be reduced by one third, what percent of the total number of employees would then be clerical?

a) 22.5%
b) 20.5%
c) 25.2%
d) 25%

Answer: d

17. A teacher wants to discuss volume measurements with her students. She asks them, how many ounces are there in one quart. What should be their answer?

a) 24 oz.
b) 12 oz.
c) 36 oz.
d) 32 oz.

Answer: d

18. What is the ratio of 1 microgram to 1 gram?

a) 0.0001 g
b) 0.00001 g
c) 0.000001 g
d) 0.0000001 g

Answer: c

19. A garden with a length of 100 meters and a width of 60 meters has a walkway of 2 meters in every side. What is the area of the garden in square meters excluding the walkway?

a) 5684

b) 6000
c) 624
d) 5376

Answer: d

20. There are 8 more men than women in a Board of Directors of a Company. If there are 20 members on the board, how many are men?

a) 6
b) 8
c) 12
d) 14

Answer: d

21. When heated, an iron bar expands 0.2% if the increased length is 1 cm, what is the original length of the bar?

a) 500 cm
b) 5 cm
c) 0.97 cm
d) 0.95 cm

Answer: a

22. A pump removes water at a rate of 600 gallons per minute. How many hours would it take to remove 1800 gallons?

a) 4 hours
b) 5 hours
c) 3 hours

d) 6 hours

23. Machine A produces bolts at a uniform rate of 120 every 40 seconds and Machine B produces bolts at a uniform rate of 100 every 20 seconds. If the two machines run simultaneously, how many seconds will it take for them to produce a total of 200 bolts?

a) 22
b) 25
c) 28
d) 32

Answer: b

24. 35% of Jason's income is equal to 25% of Harry's income. The ratio of their income is-

a) 7:5
b) 4:3
c) 4:7
d) 5:7

Answer: d

25. A pole in a pond is o.20 portions in mud, 0.50 in water and the rest 6 feet is above water. What is the length of the pole?

a) 40 feet
b) 35 feet
c) 20 feet
d) 35 feet

Answer: c

APPTITUDE

1. A farmer had 17 hens. All but 9 died, how many left?

   a) 7
   b) 3
   c) None
   d) 9

Answer: d

2. If you count 1-100, how many 5s will you pass on the way?

   a) 5
   b) 45
   c) 50
   d) 55

Answer: d

3. A and B invest in a business in the ratio 3: 2 if 5% of the profit goes to charity and A's share is $855, then how much is the total profit?

   a) $1425
   b) $1500
   c) $1300
   d) $1590

Answer: b

4. Divide 30 by half and add 10, what do you get?

a) 45
b) 35
c) 70
d) 30

Answer: c

5. If the second day of the month is a Monday, the eighteenth day of the month is?

a) Sunday
b) Friday
c) Tuesday
d) Wednesday

Answer: b

6. Today is Monday. After 61 days, it will be _____

a) Wednesday
b) Saturday
c) Tuesday
d) Friday

Answer: b

7. Mr. A is 5 years senior to Mr. B. Mr. B is 3 years senior to Mr. C. Mr. C is 2 years junior to Mr. D in job experience. If Mr. D has 15 years job experience, then how many years of experience does Mr. A possess?

a) 18
b) 19
c) 20
d) 21

8. A bus runs at 100km/h top speed. It can carry a maximum of 6 persons. If speed of bus decreases in fixed proportion, with increase in number of person, find speed when 3 persons are travelling in the bus.

a) 40km/h
b) 90km/h
c) 35km/h
d) 100km/h

9. There are 20 pieces of bread to divide among 20 people. A man eats 3 pieces, a woman eats 2 pieces and a child eats half a piece of bread. Tell the correct combination of men, women and children so that they are 20 people in total and everyone gets the bread. Note that a man cannot eat more or less than 3 pieces, a woman can't eat more or less than 2 pieces and a child cannot eat more or less than half a piece of bread. Figure out how many of those 20 people are men, women and children respectively.

a) 12 men, 2 children and 6 women
b) 11 women, 5 men and 4 children
c) 10 men, 5 women and 5 children
d) 5 women, 1 man and 14 children

10. Three people picked 65 apples altogether. At the first tree, they each picked the same number of apples. At the second tree, they each picked 3 times as many as the number of apples they picked in the first tree. When they finished the 3rd tree, the people had 5 times as many apples as they had when they started at that tree. At the fourth tree, the group picked just 5 apples. How many apples did each person pick at the first tree?

a) 5
b) 7
c) 2
d) 1

Answer: d

11. The sum of ages of 5 children born at the intervals of 3 years is 50 years. What is the age of the youngest child?

a) 4 years
b) 3 years
c) 9 years
d) None of the above

Answer: a

12. Maria's dad has 3 children. The elder son's name is- Tom, the second one is Dick, what is the third child's name?

a) Harry
b) Larry
c) Gary
d) Maria

Answer: d

13. The man sitting beside Richard is Benson. Left to Benson is Carl and right to Carl is David. Who is sitting right to Benson?

a) David
b) Carl
c) Richard
d) An unknown person

Answer: c

14. It was Sunday on January 1, 2006. What was the day of the week Jan 1, 2010?

a) Saturday
b) Sunday
c) Wednesday
d) Friday

Answer: d

15. An accurate clock shows 8 O'clock in the morning. Through how many degrees will the hour hand rotate when the clock shows 2 O'clock in the afternoon?

a) 144°
b) 150°
c) 180°
d) 168°

Answer: c

16. How many times are the hands of a clock at Right Angle in a day?

a) 44 times
b) 55 times
c) 70 times
d) Just once

Answer: a

17. Tanya is older than Ellen, Canny is older than Tanya. Ellen is older than Canny. If the first two statements are true, the third statement is-

a) True
b) False
c) Irrelevant
d) None of the above

Answer: b

18. A father said to his son- ' I was as old as you are at present at the time of your birth'. If the father's age is 38 years now , what was the son's age 5 years back?

a) 14 years
b) 19 years
c) 20 years
d) 35 years

Answer: a

19. Find the odd man out: 3,5,11,14,17,21

a) 21
b) 11
c) 3
d) 14

Answer: d

20. Which one of the following is not a prime number?

a) 71
b) 61
c) 31

d) 91

Answer: d

21. What least number must be added to 1056 so that the sum is completely divisible by 23?

a) 2
b) 18
c) 3
d) 21

Answer: a

22. In the first ten overs of a cricket game, the run rate was only 3.2 what should be the run rate in the remaining 40 overs to reach the target of 282 runs?

a) 6.25
b) 6.75
c) 6
d) 7

Answer: a

23. The average of 20 numbers is 0. Of them, at the most, how many could be greater than zero?

a) 0
b) 1
c) 10
d) 19

Answer: d

24. What decimal of an hour is a second?

a) 0.00027
b) 0.0025
c) 0.025
d) 0.000126

Answer: a

25. The product of two numbers is 120 and the sum of their squares is 289. The sum of the number is?

a) 20
b) 23
c) 139
d) 37

Answer: b

Made in the USA
Lexington, KY
08 April 2013